ALIGNED
+Alive

ALIGNED + ALIVE

Your Guide to Clarity, Self-Love, and Living with Purpose

Chrissy May

Published by Game Changer Publishing

Paperback ISBN: 978-1-963793-04-8
Hardcover ISBN: 978-1-963793-05-5
Digital ISBN: 978-1-963793-06-2

www.GameChangerPublishing.com

Dedication

This book is dedicated to my mom, who breathed life into me. My first books were about the power of kindness, acts of service, and *Bible* stories that would later escalate into personal development and the power of positive thinking. She would gift me them often, depending on what season of life I was going through. When it was a tough break-up, she would send me books on trusting in God to get through. Or when I couldn't move on, she would gift me books on codependency. If I was down and out and started second-guessing my decisions, Mom had a book for "where there is a will, there is a way." I never realized the depth of what these books have meant to me over three decades until I found a box one day in the shed filled with books from her. Ah! The long-lost box of books was finally found, and the mystery was solved. I felt the cover of each book, smiling from ear to ear as if I'd just reunited with a long-lost friend.

As I opened the books, tears started streaming down my face. Book after book, I couldn't hold back the overwhelming love my mom poured out inside each cover. Each had a date and thoughtful message—all-encompassed messages of hope, love, and support. My mom has always been my guide and sounding board. She is an extraordinary human being, one-of-a-kind. I've been blessed since she brought me home and showed me what it is to be loved. She has been my Sunday school teacher, my confidant, my therapist, my cheerleader, my driver, my chef, my banker, my nurse, and my friend.

I would not be where I am today without my mom, Mary Jo May.

Thank you for a life filled with love, cherished memories at the lake, Tennessee, family time, and long car rides with great conversations.

I love you.

"*Authentic, compassionate, empowering, a truth-seeker, a messenger. Chrissy May is all of those and more. Sharing her own personal journey that will inspire you to do the same for yourself. Chrissy has created that 'safe space' for your own self-exploration, whether it's through her podcast, coaching, her book, or a chance meeting with her. A breath of fresh air.*"

- Jenna DiGiuseppi, IHAP, RMT Sacred Pause Healing

"*Chrissy is deeply devoted to the path of transformation and personal development. The most trustable allies and guides are those who embark on their own path of remembrance and becoming with all of their hearts and Chrissy is absolutely in that category. She embodies her commitment to self-love, and you can too!*"

- Maria Teresa Chavez, Evolutionary relationship coach, medicine woman and mentor

"*Chrissy May is an absolute light being whose life is a testament to the power of self-love, compassion, and purposeful living. Her dedication to helping others, including myself, shines a light of transformation and possibility the moment you connect with her. Chrissy has dedicated her resources and time to finding tools we need as she has guided countless individuals to practice self-love and compassion at the deepest level. Chrissy's book is a step-by-step guide that encapsulates her mission to add value to every single person she can. This book is her gift to the world, and it reflects the same depth of care and insight that she brings to her personal interactions and retreats.*"

- Robin Kimery, Hypnotherapist

ALIGNED + Alive

*Your Guide to Clarity, Self-Love,
and Living with Purpose*

Chrissy May

 GAME CHANGER
PUBLISHING

www.GameChangerPublishing.com

Table of Contents

Introduction

What to expect from this book? I am providing a blueprint that will shift you into spiritual alignment, increase clarity and self-love, help you build confidence, heighten your intuition, and allow you to become a magnet for greater wealth, health, and abundance. We attract who we are, not what we want, so creating a daily routine that resonates with your soul's truth is essential. Once you decide to immerse yourself in your growth and spiritual journey, you will be on your way to living a life full of meaning and purpose. We become whole and complete when we consistently show up for ourselves. Thank you for allowing me to be a part of your journey, the best ride you will ever be on, and for becoming who you are meant to be during this human experience.

For the beautiful soul ready to shift into a new reality—a new way of being without feeling blocked or limited from their past, ready to live out their next chapter with greater clarity, conviction, and ease, this book will provide you an opportunity to connect deeper with yourself and gain the strength to take inspired action.

I am a former competitive athlete and people pleaser turned personal development, self-love specialist. My journey of struggle to self-discovery has allowed me to show up for others as a facilitator for alignment. I've had the privilege and honor of helping women and men from all walks of life throughout my twenty-two years of experience in the health and wellness industry.

As a serial entrepreneur for my entire adult life, I've worn and still wear many hats: real estate advisor and investor, owning and operating brick-and-mortar health and wellness small businesses in Arizona, I've created and launched over two dozen brands and business concepts since 1998, held an editor-in-chief position for a local publication, I've been published in over a dozen health and fitness publications since 1999, have hosted celebrity red carpet events, appeared on TV shows, handful of movies, competed in Fitness America Pageants and trained as a competitive figure skater for ten years. Yes, it's been a colorful life that allows me to serve clients at a high level in their personal and professional lives.

Besides the many ventures, one of my deepest passions is podcasting. *Aligned + Alive Podcast with Chrissy May* launched on June 22, 2022, a platform that allows me to connect with humans worldwide and create meaningful relationships. As I write this book, it is currently ranked as a top 1% podcast worldwide. We discuss health, wellness, spirituality, and mindset topics, allowing you to become connected, aligned, and fully alive! Information on how to download and listen to my podcast will be available at the end of this book. I have over twenty-two guided meditations you can use and many valuable episodes that will enrich your life.

When you allow yourself to go within and explore, monumental shifts can take place. For example, maybe you are holding onto resentment from past hurt or can't let go of attachments that are making you sick—emotionally and physically. When you are ready to open up and do the inner work, you will experience a life beyond your wildest imagination, full of love, bliss, and abundance. It's waiting for you; all you have to do is remain committed throughout the process. Lead with an open mind, remain curious, and watch the miracle unfold. If you follow these steps, it's impossible not to experience a new reality, a new way of being filled with clarity, self-love, and living with purpose.

Miracles

"You are the God who
performs miracles."
- *Psalm 77:14*

Chapter 1

MIRACLE BEGINNINGS

I was driving home from a party late one night in the summer of 1993. All windows were down as the beautiful breeze blew around my sun-kissed blonde hair. I felt free, as any 16-year-old would, having recently been issued my driver's license. Not a care in the world other than making sure I hit my 11:00 p.m. curfew on time. I arrived shortly after, a tad past 11:15. As luck would not have it, my mom had locked the front door, which was my only way in, forcing me to ring the doorbell as I conveniently forgot my house key. The smirk I tried to hold back on my face didn't warm my mother's heart but rather infuriated her, not to mention having to answer her question, "Have you had anything to drink?" I told her I was attending a bonfire, and some kids brought a keg of beer, a typical setting in the middle of cornfields in suburban Illinois. She asked again, as I didn't answer the first time, which quickly was followed up with, "Give me your car keys; you are grounded." Only two months into my young adulthood, I was already getting my newfound freedom stripped away. This marked the beginning of some "troubling" years with my mother. I constantly pushed limits, and she always reprimanded me for my free-spirited behavior.

Let's Go Back to the Very Beginning

The year was 1977. Jimmy Carter was sworn in as the 39th President of the United States. NASA launched Voyager 1 and 2 from Kennedy Space Center and traveled to explore the outer planets. The Apple 2 computer was introduced. The average annual income was $15,000. A gallon of gas cost 65 cents. The King of Rock and Roll, Mr. Elvis Presley, died of a heart attack at the tender young age of 42, and the most predominant religion was Catholicism, at over 83%, which is a crucial point in this story; remember that statistic.

My parents, Wayne and Mary Jo, were married in 1972. They had their first child, my brother Tim, in 1973. They unsuccessfully tried for a second child not long after, but my mom's physician told her that she had reproductive issues, so the chances of her having another child were extremely low.

In the summer of 1977, they explored the adoption route and met with a social worker at the Children's Home and Aid Society in Chicago, Illinois. Apparently, there was a two-year waiting list, which, again, did not defeat their spirits. Following the application process, the social worker said she would be in touch when a child became available.

A week passed, and they received a phone call that a miraculous event occurred. A young girl just dropped off a 3-month-old baby, and her only request was that she be placed with a Catholic family. Out of 22 people on the waitlist, they were the only ones who were Catholic, bumping them up from 22 to number one. Ecstatic to meet their new bundle of joy, they rushed downtown, putting their Tennessee trip on hold. They were warned that the baby had been neglected, was extremely malnourished, and cried constantly, so to their surprise, when they opened the door, they were met with a huge smile and sparkling blue eyes as if the baby girl knew *her* miracle had arrived.

My mom and dad swiftly picked me up, brought me back to our suburban home, and fattened me up. Three years later, in 1980, my mom would receive another miracle and naturally deliver a healthy baby girl, my younger sister Cindy—making me the middle yet still favorite child. *(laughing)*

Ever since I was a little girl, I felt overwhelming love and gratitude. My mom always made me feel special. I came to learn of my adoption through our bedtime prayers one night when she told me how they "picked" me. After a minute or two of asking several questions so I could understand what she meant, I quickly correlated that with her not having to gain weight and go through the pain of labor with me as she did with the other two, so I always felt like the "star child." All humor aside, I never felt like the "adopted one," other than that, I stood out with my bright blonde hair and blue eyes in contrast to their dark hair and green eyes.

I reflect on my childhood with a whole, happy heart. While our family was far from perfect, it was consistent, loving, stable, and adventurous. Raised by two middle-class conservatives, my mom, who is a devout Christian raised in Illinois, stayed home to raise us. In contrast, my dad, a simple farm boy raised in Tennessee, worked as a crane and steel engineer setting steel for many high rises in downtown Chicago. We were far from rich by monetary standards but always seemed to have more than enough. Private schooling, boating on the lake all summer, family vacations, engaging in all sports activities—including my passion for nearly ten years, figure skating.

The Need to Know More

Around 8, I began asking more questions about my adoption. By this time, I was a natural seeker, constantly asking questions, needing to know more, and not settling for one-sentence answers in all areas of life. I wanted to dig deeper. I wasn't mad, angry, or resentful one bit, yet I was utterly curious. Questions that arose in me were: *What does my birth mother look like? Why did she give me up? Do I have other siblings?*

I presented these questions to my mom, who gave me more information than I could have hoped for. In the hallway of my parents' house, there is an antique chest that belonged to my great-great-grandmother on my mom's side, dating back to the 1800s. I've always loved that piece of furniture and the antique dishes behind the glass. Inside, there is a secret compartment under a mini drawer.

When I turned 10, my mom walked me over to it and opened it. She pulled out a small piece of paper with cursive writing on the front and back. I immediately knew it was her writing. She said, "I knew this time would come, and you would want answers. When we picked you up, I wrote as much information down from your file at the children's home." I had butterflies in my stomach. I couldn't wait to put all my questions and curiosity to rest.

I eagerly read the words she wrote and learned of my birth mother's name—which will become another vital part of this story later on—I learned the basic information of her height, weight, and background and eventually read the last part, my birth father. I never really gave much thought to him; I didn't care. Oddly enough, I didn't picture her with anyone, and I was raised in a family where it was the norm to be married to have a child.

As I continued to read, I learned it was an affair that had been ongoing for five years. He was much older than her and had two kids and a wife. My heart sank, not because of him, but because of how I was conceived. The story was elaborated further by the social worker who interviewed my birth mother at adoption, that she tried to keep me to keep him, yet he went back to his wife and kids. She did not know how to care for me, even at 20. Many friends and family members would tell her to give me up, as I had not been fed for days on end by her. Neighbors would come in to change my dirty diapers and give me a bottle.

Eventually, as you know, she gave in, and I couldn't be more grateful for her decision. It could have gone many other ways, but I believe God guided her that day, knowing she had to make right with all that had transpired.

The Search is On

Fast forward to 1989. *Jerry Springer, Sally Jessy Raphael,* and *Oprah* are daytime's biggest shows, and I was watching! They were notorious for posting info at the end of shows on "adoption search." I immediately put on my investigator's hat and went to work. The show's "search" fee was $67 plus tax, so I purchased a money order, mailed in my information, and hoped they would find my birth mother. Yes, I fell for it. Weeks and months passed with nothing but silence. My hard-earned babysitting money was gone. (I feel like Ralphie from *A Christmas Story* while writing this. LOL.)

Years went by with no thought of my adoption or the questions I initially posed. I shifted my focus to figure skating, working out in the gym, and school. As a high school sophomore, I tried out for the cheerleading squad and divided my time between skating and extracurricular activities. This is one of those flashback moments in the movies where you pause the screen and caption it with, *"What if I never went this route?"* I believe my life would have put me on a completely different trajectory. However, I would not have learned many valuable life lessons from this period. This would be one of the most painful and confusing moments of my teenage years, yet it would also serve as the precursor to my massive growth many years later.

In the summer of 1999, I finally left Illinois and moved to Arizona. I yearned for a change and a new direction. I instinctively knew I could no longer stay in my hometown if I wanted to create a healthier life for myself. I enrolled in a degree and many certificate programs at the Southwest Institute of Healing Arts and began a new way of life that filled me with so much meaning and purpose. I finally felt connected for the first time in my life. I loved learning everything about the mind, body, spirit, and healing disease in the body, not masking it. I would open my health and fitness company a few short years later.

Moving to Arizona would become one of the best decisions I've ever made and one of the most transformative. I remember so vividly seeing Sedona for the first time. All my sensory units were fired when I turned off the 89 freeway and drove through the Red Rock region. It's as if I had been there before. I felt connected, supported, and aligned. Sedona had my heart at first sight—it is an extraordinary place for me. It would be the first time I experienced energy healing and knew what I have always felt—we are much more powerful than we know. It was an extraordinary time shedding the old, leaving behind all that didn't serve me, and stepping boldly into a new chapter.

After moving to Arizona, I realized that environment plays an even more significant part in *who* and *what* you become. You need to immerse yourself in energies and environments that allow you to expand and grow, environments that ignite a feeling that you cannot get in a stagnated place. It's essential to recognize your inner feelings, calling you to a higher standard in life. Don't label it good or bad; it's just a calling, and when it hits, you must take action. It's your soul's purpose whispering to you. It's here, many years down the road, that I would also revive my adoption investigation and ultimately find my extended birth family.

God is in Everything—Notice the Winks When They Appear

As you now have learned, the number 22 holds special meaning for me, beginning with my adoption story. I was also 22 when I left my hometown and drove across the country to begin a new and exciting chapter of my life. Yet it was also a time of questioning, searching, and learning more about myself as I navigated the alternative path before me. At 22, I began working with a faith-based spiritual counselor and intuitive named Halina, who would help me cultivate my intuition and guide me along my spiritual journey. I will never forget our first session together.

From the moment I first looked into her eyes, I felt we had known each other for a lifetime. She grabbed my hands, recited a prayer, and told me about my adoption at three months old. She explained how she saw a young girl dropping me off at a children's home as she could no longer care for me. My eyes grew and grew as she continued. All I remember thinking was, *How does she know this? I've never met her. I don't know anyone in Arizona, nor does anyone know the details of my adoption but my parents.* Halina further explained how there were many babies in front of me to be adopted. She was right. As I shared earlier, I was number 22 on the list, yet because my birth mother specifically asked that I be placed with a Catholic family, I was bumped up to number 1.

As I write this book, another unique experience occurred recently: the divine gift of a sweet female boxer we rescued from Love Pup dog rescue in Phoenix, Arizona, now named Halo. She was in horrible shape with a terrible case of "valley fever," sores in her eyes from stress, and her spine protruding out of her back from lack of nourishment. She was as close to death as possible, yet was saved by compassionate individuals who moved her away from her abuser and into Love Pup. When the adoption became official, I glanced at her medical records and cried. *She was born on January 22nd.* There is no doubt in my mind that God loves to send me winks, and when it happens in the form of the number 22, it brings a massive smile to my face, as you can imagine. My entry into this world was a perfectly orchestrated miracle from the beginning; regardless of how it happened, it all happened for a reason.

I've found that when I am in alignment, leaning into my faith, and letting go, all unfolds the way it should. If I operate out of fear or ego, I block the messages that want to come through. As I trust the process of what is meant for my highest and best good, life becomes a connected and meaningful playground. My foundation is my faith. I am not imposing my beliefs onto you throughout this book, but merely inviting you into my story and sharing my life experiences of what I have been through to where I am today. I work with clients from all walks of life and belief systems. (Insert your higher power or belief in relation to mine for a more personal experience if needed throughout this book.)

Even if you came from an unhealthy environment, somewhere along the way, you were presented with a wink or two.

love,
love,
love

"How you love yourself
is how you teach others
to love you."
- *Rupi Kaur*

Chapter 2

SELF-LOVE IS THE GREATEST LOVE

As a former people pleaser with low self-worth, I can say with certainty that my greatest accomplishment to date is the ability to love and fully show up for myself daily, but it took me years to get here! I wish I could say it was easy peasy, but there were many messy moments along the way. Much of my life was self-sacrificing. This is how I learned to receive love. The more I gave and did for others, the greater the praise. Unfortunately, by living this way, I suffered internally and in silence. This would go on for many years until I began to slowly implement a self-care practice that took me many years to master. It doesn't have to take you that long because I can provide all the tools and techniques to spring you into a delicious state of self-love.

If you don't place a high value on yourself, others likely won't either unless it aligns with their agenda. I quickly saw the patterns play out in my daily reflection meditations. I could hear the whispers from God and knew exactly what I needed to do—knowing and doing are two completely different things. It's never easy heading into the unknown, yet when you have faith and connection, you understand that all will work out in your favor. Obstacles now become opportunities, and that gut-wrenching feeling in the pit of your stomach softens as you release attachments and breathe, knowing that a miracle is taking place.

I like to shift my perspective in any uncomfortable situation and remind myself that this is an opportunity to elevate and everything I have gone through until now has prepared me for this moment, so I choose to sit in the feeling of excitement rather than fear. This shift is another excellent way to infuse self-love and build your self-worth. When we exercise complete love for ourselves, mountains move, and people, situations, and opportunities appear. I've created a list of my "go-to" practices to deepen self-love.

Contrary to what you may have seen on social media, it's not all bubble baths and big shopping sprees. These steps will nurture, support, and empower you from within. Something money can't buy.

6 Simple Steps to Self-Love

1. Do What You Say You Will Do - The quickest way to build confidence and self-worth, which goes hand-in-hand with self-love, is to show up and keep your commitments. When you keep promises, you build trust in yourself. This reliability forms the foundation of self-confidence because you prove to yourself that you are capable and dependable. Following through on your commitments demonstrates integrity and consistency. These qualities not only enhance how you view yourself but also how others perceive you, reinforcing positive feedback loops that boost self-esteem. When you see yourself as someone who follows through, you develop a more positive self-image. This positive self-image is crucial for self-love because it shapes how you treat yourself and what you believe you deserve. So when you say you are going to do something, no matter how insignificant it may seem, follow through with your word, it will serve you in more ways than you can imagine throughout your lifetime. It builds trust in yourself and those interacting with you. When you learn to trust yourself fully, you allow space to love yourself completely. You create a foundation for respect, and life will respond to your personal standard.

2. Set Healthy Boundaries - This step will become your best friend. Learning how to create the courage to follow through and impose this step will revisit the first, doing what you say you will do. To enforce setting healthy boundaries, one must master the ability to show up for oneself. This step becomes impossible if you can't even follow through on your word. When you build self-worth, you build self-love; when you build self-love, you respect yourself more, allowing you the strength and courage to show up and enforce a personal standard. Your standards will ultimately dictate what kind of life you will lead.

No matter what transpires around you, your standard of acceptance and what you tolerate in your energy will decide how you feel and choose to see the world. Keeping toxic individuals in your company will spill over into your energy and create a sense of chaos within you. So when you feel overwhelmed and know it's not you, this is your sign to clean up what and who you allow into your space.

Often, this involves close loved ones, which can be extremely challenging to navigate. However, if you honor and respect yourself, you can have that necessary conversation to shift the narrative and move into a space that elevates the connection for all involved. Setting boundaries won't cost you real friends and relationships. It will shine a light on who is not in alignment with your values. There are five general boundary categories: physical, emotional, sexual, mental, and financial. To establish effective personal boundaries, you have to know what your core values and beliefs are in the first place, then learn to communicate those clearly and effectively while also sharing what the consequences would be if those are violated. Boundaries are healthy limits that allow you space to thrive.

3. Honor your Body - Respect it as a holy temple and sacred ground. Cherish every inch with love and kindness. It wasn't until I was in my late 30s that I recognized why I allowed self-sabotage to rule my life for so long. I had so much inner work to do. We can often mask the darkest situations with more than the harmful obvious. Even healthy obsessions can be used to cover up and cope with trauma. I speak transparently when I say the only way through the pain is to release all that is not serving your highest and best good. Tear down the walls, allowing for shame, guilt, and suffering to fall away. Feel it and move through it. To shift through deep states of self-sabotage and abuse, I had to surrender to every ounce of pain I had been carrying through all the years.

Eventually, forgiveness became my best friend and allowed for the ultimate release. From this state, I could honor myself, love, and respect the innocent soul who entered this world decades ago, before all the programming began. Proper nutrition, environment, and intimate partners will all be crucial. I have experienced what it's like not to honor your body, and my life became a reflection of that for a period. I attracted relationships that didn't respect me because I lacked self-respect.

When I began to heal and elevate my life, situations and the people I attracted also shifted. Certain relationships disappeared, creating space for new and healthy situations to unfold. Honoring yourself will ultimately determine what quality of life you will experience. Be compassionate with your sacred vessel; nurture it with love and gratitude. If you choose to imbibe in alcohol, drugs, processed foods, sugar, chemicals of any kind, understand those all suck life out of your body. Fuel it mindfully with nourishing, whole organic foods and clean filtered water. I view nutrition vastly differently than I did years ago.

When I was a fitness model and competitor in my early days of competing, the end goal was simple: get as lean as possible. Ten percent body fat was glorified, yet how we arrived there wasn't always "healthy." I quickly learned that most "healthy" contest prep was an oxymoron. It wasn't until I began training with the late Charles Poliquin, an Olympic Strength and Conditioning Coach, that I would learn how to eat natural foods that provide nutrients to my body, which gave me a more significant result without sucking the life out of it. When the facts become apparent, the choices become obvious. Give life to your body, and you will experience a life of abundance.

4. Spend Time in Nature - Daily meditation walks or hikes in nature can heal you in the most challenging times and provide unwavering love and support. Walking helps reduce inflammation and boosts your immune system. Unplug, leave your device at home or in your pocket, and don't look at it, and allow yourself to be and listen to all of God's magnificent creation: the birds chirping, the wind blowing on your face, the smell of fresh cut grass or the rustling of the leaves. When I began shedding the layers of subconscious pain I had been harboring, nature became my saving grace. I have had many walks in nature where I can recall when I would sob like a baby, which ultimately served as a much-needed release. Prayer, gratitude, and appreciation would overtake me, and I could feel God's hand renewing my soul.

I immersed myself further in these healing walks even more when my dad passed on in August 2022. My mom was simultaneously diagnosed with late-stage cancer, leaving our family gutted at the thought of losing both of our parents within months of each other. Mom, being the warrior and devout Christian she is, fought the most brutal battle of her life, supported by her mighty prayer team, and ultimately defeated the nasty disease that was ravaging her frail frame.

Anyone who has lost a parent or watched a loved one go through cancer treatments understands the toll it can take on your health and well-being. The stress, overwhelm, sadness, anger, anxiety, whatever surfaces, can have a profound effect on your physical and mental state. Nature walks and my daily conversations with God carried me through one of the most challenging seasons of my life. It's fitting that nature would become a saving grace for introspection and provide me with greater self-love.

The power of creation supports us and heals us in times of need. When you practice nurturing in nature daily, you tap into an abundant source that feeds your soul. I use this as an exploration process as well. I love uncovering unknown places, which brings me to meet new people. The benefits are plenty, which evoke a sense of wonder and curiosity. It is a fast-track way to fall in love with self.

5. Mirror Work - How do you talk to yourself? This has to be one of the most overlooked steps to self-love. Do you constantly compare yourself to others? Do you find it hard to accept compliments and praise? And a common one, do you say "sorry" 99% of the time? We need to reframe your verbiage if you answered "yes" to any of these. An exercise I began using several years ago is called "mirror work." This practice was created by transformational teacher and self-love expert, Louise Hay. Certain psychological principles and studies explain why mirror work positively affects many individuals.

The Self-Perception Theory suggests that individuals develop their self-concept by observing their behavior and making conclusions about their attitudes and feelings. It's a reflective opportunity to see yourself positively, reinforcing a more favorable self-perception. This aids in changing negative thought patterns and contributes to neural changes that support a more positive self-image. It's a simple way to cultivate self-compassion while gazing in the mirror, stating positive affirmations, such as "I am beautiful and strong," "I can achieve my heart's desires," and "I am worthy," to give you a few examples. When I began this practice many years ago, it initially felt strange to stare at myself while proclaiming statements, yet, oh my goodness, how powerfully it worked!

I encourage you to give this one a go! Peel away the fear and self-judgment and begin seeing the beauty and truth of your heart. Commit to a 22-day practice, and you will feel lighter and more empowered. I will provide additional insight into the power of your thoughts and the words you speak in Chapter 7.

6. Progress Over Perfection - Give yourself some grace. The last thing you want is to focus on what is lacking or not going right. It goes against this entire process of building self-love, only for you to tear it all down. It is like someone who works hard to get in top shape, only to eat potato chips again every day. We are training another muscle, your brain and heart coherence, creating harmony. Research shows that when you shift into a coherent state, the heart and brain operate synergistically, meshing into one system. When these systems are not in balance, you may experience stress, anxiety, and even depression. Focus on your progress and speak your truth through the mirror work I mentioned in the above step.

Your job is to only pay attention to how you show up for yourself, focusing on the progress being made, you will then begin to embody every bit of this new way of living. When training as a skater on the ice for several hours a day, five days a week, you can only imagine the falls I took while learning new jumps, spins, and footwork. Frankly, it's more than I can count and even wrap my mind around! There were many days I would go home with my right side entirely bruised from all the hits to the ice. Yet, for every dozen falls I took, there was that one perfect execution of an element that kept me coming back for more. I now had proof that I could perform and execute at a high level; it just took consistently showing up and practicing. I focused on my progress, which allowed me to eventually master specific skills. Don't give up, no matter how hard things get.

"Fall 7 times, stand up 8." - A Japanese proverb.

Clarity

"Don't dance around the perimeter of the person you want to be. Dive deeply and fully into it."
- *Gabrielle Bernstein*

Chapter 3

CLARITY BRINGS ALIGNED AND INSPIRED ACTION

Clarity allows you to focus and take action! When you aren't clear on your goals and personal standards, you fall into a state of self-doubt, overwhelm, and indecisiveness, ultimately creating chaos in life as mental and emotional confusion. While you may not experience it all at once, it will eventually creep up on you, leaving you feeling stuck and stagnant. As the late Zig Ziglar once said, "Don't become a wandering generality, be a meaningful specific." Many who lack clarity in their lives often confuse "busy" with being productive. It doesn't take much to move through the motions daily; observe the general population, and most operate on autopilot. You may be one of these people, and that's okay, but it's time to interrupt the pattern and become clear so you can show up with intentionality and begin living a life with purpose. Getting clear will allow you to create and effortlessly align with your heart's desires while providing empowerment and the ability to navigate life with greater ease and discernment. The power of clarity provides you the space to become the best version of yourself and the ability to squeeze the most out of life.

I worked with a man in his 40s many years ago when I had my health and fitness company. He was going through an ugly divorce with a woman who had verbally abused him and beat him down emotionally until he had no self-worth remaining. It was my first time experiencing this with a male. Most of my clients enrolled in my empowerment program were female, and many had the same unfortunate story, yet also included physical abuse. Seeing his empty eyes as he recounted the years of turmoil was heartbreaking. He was highly successful financially. His then-wife acted like a bully at an elementary school playground, unleashing a power on him like no other. While working closely with his licensed therapist, I was asked to create an empowerment program for him. We met three times a week for several months.

I had him journaling before and after our sessions together, working through repressed emotions, and building him back up in ways many people don't think about with physical activity. My fitness center had several oversized tractor tires that I had clients flip and use sledgehammers to pound with incredible force. During this phase, he would shout words of affirmation with each blow stemming from his inner strength. I would also ask him questions during this exercise, and he would answer with conviction as he pounded away. Many of you reading this may think it sounds harsh or over the top, yet this is precisely what this man needed during this time: to rebuild, to show up and do hard things, to dig deep from within and tap into that power that we all have been given, yet somewhere along the journey it was stripped away from years of abuse and negative programming. With each slam to the tire weekly, I witnessed a broken soul who could barely speak to an empowered man who stood tall and confident, ready to begin a new and exciting chapter of his life with unwavering clarity and conviction. It was the first time he ever felt a sense of peace.

While his healing journey continued for many months, he experienced a profound shift in what he called "a miracle transformation." He allowed himself to feel the pain, move through it with great tenacity, and remain curious. It's hard to trust the process when you aren't clear, and as he became more apparent, how he showed up became more accessible and manageable. I helped him refocus by using a method that works for many: "Minimize to maximize." I narrowed down his lifestyle on what mattered most and created a plan that would allow him only to entertain what was meant for his highest and best good during this difficult time. Many years later, I still use this method with my clients with a slight twist, as we now have social media outlets that can affect our mental and emotional well-being.

Implement these three steps to master clarity and get into alignment.

The 3 Rs (Remove, Reconnect, Reflect): A Discovery Process to Align Your Life

1. REMOVE: Many people don't even realize what they need to remove from their environment or what is really distracting them in the first place, creating that sense of chaos and overwhelm in their lives. In this step, it's time to take a serious inventory of your life. Every detail is down to what you allow your eyes to see, what you allow your ears to hear, what you allow your mouth to eat, what you allow your body to experience, and who you allow in your space daily. Every action and choice you make moves you toward an abundant life or away from it. Removing what is taking you away will create space for higher vibrational energy, people, and situations that will allow you to elevate and grow.

The saying "Starve your distractions and feed your focus" couldn't be more perfectly stated. Take your journal and write what distracts you from showing up and getting clear. It could be a bad habit, a toxic person, or an environment stifling and keeping you stuck. You may consume harmful content on social media, YouTube, and the news or scrolling aimlessly. All can lead to anxiety, uneasiness, fear, and a myriad of other disorders that will continue to cloud your perception. This is the time to be completely honest with yourself and take ownership! What we allow will only persist. You are 100% the problem for allowing it to continue, yet you are also 100% the solution to shift the course of your trajectory. Become intentional with your time during this process.

Dr. Bruce Lipton began his career as a cell biologist, graduating from the University of Virginia before joining the Department of Anatomy at the University of Wisconsin's School of Medicine in 1973. Today, he describes his work as bridging science and spirituality, and in his bestselling book *The Biology of Belief*, he states, "Our thoughts and environment affect all the cells in our body." Think about that. When you are experiencing a lack of clarity, the many thoughts in your mind are typically erratic and often assumption-based. False beliefs take over, forming into limiting beliefs. So, the lack of clarity, coupled with the buzzing of negative thought patterns forming, is now affecting all the cells in your body! You are becoming confused and uncertain on a cellular level, which suppresses your immune system.

Now, let's shift to your environment. For example, you have the news playing in the background, covering homicides, war, and government issues while you make dinner. Or maybe you are innocently watching a TV show that has guns going off every minute, fight scenes, or vulgar language—you get my point? These low vibrational environmental stressors are seeping into your subconscious mind, also suppressing you at the cellular level. So, let me ask you, how do you plan on creating a life you love, reaping the rewards of a high-vibrational, positive environment when you allow the noise and distractions in the background to play out? It can't be done. It will influence you. This is where you must become super intentional with your entire life, specifically your environment. The energy you are in will influence your environment just as the environment you are in will influence your energy. They are interchangeable.

Dr. Lipton explains how, as children, our subconscious minds "download" what we see and hear everyone around us doing and saying, and these become the programs that drive our habits and thinking throughout life. Depending on our experiences, they might be programs like, "I'm not good enough" or "It's my fault." A common one for many was, "Money doesn't grow on trees." You can see how these might create unwanted behaviors as we grow up. It's time to grab hold of the wheel to create an environment to set you up for success. Instead of a TV show, opt for a calm, beautiful playlist or a motivational podcast to help encourage a healthier lifestyle. Remove anything that is not adding value to your life daily. When working from home, I position myself outside (weather permitting) to feel the fresh air and sun beaming down on me. My mood is instantly in a better place. I'm creating an inspired, soothing environment, priming me for the day with zero distractions.

2. RECONNECT: When we "lose" ourselves and feel clouded in judgment, we have lost connection to self. This is because of the many distractions that are pulling at us daily, which is precisely why I have that as the first step in this process. Over time, this will stack in an unfavorable direction and path for your future if you don't nip it immediately. By connecting back to self and nurturing your overall well-being, you can show up in ways you never thought possible. Take a pause, a moment to breathe, and experience the magic that lies within you.

I use many modalities to reconnect; the key is to find what aligns with you. Breathwork, meditation, sound healing, earthing/grounding, prayer, nature, and the ocean are valuable resources for connecting, aligning, and feeling fully alive! I have spent the last two decades of my life working on myself. It is a lifelong journey and the best one you will ever be on. You are exploring what is possible when you peel back the onion and shed the layers individually. Through reconnecting with self, anything is possible, my friend, anything! You deepen self-love, which is essential in getting clear on your vision, goals and navigating life's many peaks and valleys. When you trust yourself fully, the confidence and connection you gain will magnetize situations and opportunities that now align with your current state of being. It's impossible not to. Connection to self is vital. This now allows you to show up in your whole authentic truth. Not what your family, friends, or society tells you how to be, yet how you are, tapping into your complete potentiality. Do you even know how powerful you are?

Commit to a daily practice of connection to self and feel the magical shift transform before your eyes. This isn't "woo-woo." This is tuning out the noise and disruption so you can fully align. I love taking meditation and visualization walks in nature. They pop me right back into the present moment, where your point of power lies. Connecting to self offers a multitude of additional benefits, including increased self-awareness, improved emotional and mental well-being, enhanced relationships with others and fostering healthier connections, builds resilience, allowing you to bounce back from setbacks as you understand yourself and capabilities better, reduces stress, sparks creativity and productivity and provides you the ability to make better decisions that are in alignment with your values.

A quick method to use when reconnecting to self is to focus solely on gratitude. What are you grateful for? Maybe it's that you can read this book and learn more to move closer to a life you love. Or that you have another day of life to rewrite your story and create a new narrative. I offer these two simple ones for those struggling to find beauty when life isn't going how they'd like.

We all go through unpleasant seasons of life. When my dad passed away in August 2022, it was a pain I never experienced, piercing through every cell of my body. I cried uncontrollably for what seemed like hours. After I moved through that initial shock and extreme sadness, I focused on the fact that I had experienced a long life with him, and I was so grateful for our time together. This didn't remove my pain entirely, yet it brought me a greater sense of peace in that moment and allowed me to shift back to connection with myself almost immediately. I could reframe my thoughts and emotions after moving through the initial wave of grief. I could sit in the present moment, which guided me along the way. Coming back to self is our saving grace.

3. REFLECT: Each day, set aside 10-15 minutes to observe where you are currently along the journey. This takes complete self-awareness. Be bold and honest with yourself so you can make

adjustments if needed. Maybe there are areas you are thriving in and others you are still stuck in. That's okay! This is not the time to beat yourself up and throw in the towel; it's a time to build upon your self-awareness and pivot if needed. Be kind to yourself. One cannot grow in dried-out dirt; it needs water and nutrients to flourish. You are human; shift your mindset to progress, not perfection. Remind yourself that you are amazing, unique, and beautiful; that is your power! It's time to show up and stand in it like the bright, shining star you were born to be, regardless of your current situation. Reflection gives us permission to keep showing up while refining our goals. Reflection plays a pivotal role in deepening clarity. When you take time to reflect, you allow your mind to process experiences, thoughts, and emotions. You gain insights into your patterns of behavior. It allows you to observe challenges from different angles, potentially revealing new perspectives and solutions.

Ultimately, this process serves as a tool for self-discovery and understanding, allowing you to navigate life with increased clarity and purpose. It's a process that unfolds over time, continually aiding your personal development and enhancing the quality of your decisions and actions. I love sitting and writing in my comfy chair next to the fireplace or outside as the sun sets. I use this moment to clarify what went well and worked and what isn't going according to plan. I see the solution almost instantly 99.99% of the time. Though it may not be what I want to admit, it's a solution. Then, what I do with that moment of reflection is entirely up to me.

This is where many experience a block of action. We may gain extreme clarity on a person, experience, or environment and still do nothing about it because it's hard and uncomfortable. This is where you continually circle back to the top of this list and begin again, sharpening your skillset. You will become more refined as you work with the "3 Rs." I spend a lot of my time reconnecting to self (step number 2) because I know the more I can connect with who I am (my authentic truth), and learning to stand in my power, taking action that aligns with my core values and beliefs becomes seamless.

My Personal Story From Abuse to Overcomer

For you to understand more clearly how I could create such a successful program for my clients who experienced emotional and physical abuse, it was because I went through it myself. I have never used the words "victim" or "survivor" as they never resonated with me, so I will not be referencing them. I've often reflected upon this moment as a "gift" in order to help serve others in their own healing journey.

Many years ago, in my late twenties, I dated a highly charismatic, good-looking, fit, intelligent man from a prominent East Coast family. He checked all the boxes for sure, or so I thought. It wasn't long into our relationship that I felt something was off. The mask faded away, and I received signs that his picture-perfect life wasn't what he initially presented. I learned of his abuse as a child and former drug addiction, and I would later come to find that he was still in that addiction but had been hiding it from me the entire time. I received confirmation from my mom, who met him when I brought him back for a weekend trip to Illinois. I will never forget her words, "Chrissy, he is a nice man, but something is off."

After meeting him, most of my friends agreed. Eventually, I tried to break away from the relationship only to find myself back in it, mainly out of fear. I still look back on that moment in my life with sadness. I can't relate to that young woman who allowed such a man into her precious life, yet I understand why, now that I have had fifteen years of healing, growing, and evolving to where I am today.

The abuse didn't start until the very end when I was trying to muster the courage to leave him once and for all. The arguments were heightened, and I constantly felt I was in survival mode until one horrific night made me wake up. He didn't seem right when he picked me up from a New Year's Eve party. He told me he wasn't drinking or taking drugs any longer, yet I could now see the pattern and knew he was lying. I eventually stood up to him and told him I was done. He gripped my throat and threw me against the kitchen wall. The abuse continued until the wee hours of the morning. I tried to leave and call for help, but he took my phone and blocked me from leaving—there was only one way in and out. He finally passed out, and I grabbed my phone and called for help. This would begin my healing journey, and it wasn't easy sailing.

I learned a lot about myself through my therapy sessions, but therapy wasn't enough. I began writing programs on how I could eventually move through this challenging period without continuing to mask the pain and fall deeper into a pit of despair. I shifted my mind from the experience, and my experience changed. I had the necessary knowledge and skillset; the challenge now was consistently applying them every day. I knew my experience resulted from not having a high personal standard.

Reflecting on that period, I can see that the younger me had little self-worth. It is impossible to allow an unhealthy attachment to continue when you embody self-love and create a higher standard of living. That 27-year-old me had neither, so it isn't surprising that my fate unfolded the way it did during that moment in my life. We must take 100% ownership of our life choices and the choice to become healthier from the inside out. We must commit to digging deep and heal so we may respect ourselves, which will not allow for any such abuse to take place.

Wherever you find yourself along your journey, understand there is always a gift to receive. Mine was, *"Thank you, God, for this life experience so I may learn to love myself and trust in you more fully."* God allows our life choices to unfold the way they may, with free will, so we may choose again and become the greatest version of ourselves. Choice is the one constant we all share. I never promised it would be easy, but I do promise anything is possible. My life is a living testament. We all can pivot out of the darkness and back into the light. You don't need to stay stuck.

Gabrielle Bernstein is a world-renowned spiritual leader and #1 *New York Times* multi-best-selling author. I hold her in high regard and credit her for much of my healing over the years. Gabby often emphasizes the significance of clarity as a driving force for transformation, empowerment, and living a purposeful life. Her quotes reflect the idea that we can achieve our aspirations with confidence and determination when we have clarity.

Here are a few "Gabby Quotes" that have served as beautiful reminders:

"Much of our anxiety and stress comes when we're focused on fear and disconnected from the voice of our inner guide."

"I will let no one walk through my mind with their dirty feet."

"Today, I no longer need to change the world around me. I need to change."

"I'm ready to learn through love."

"I affirm I am worthy."

"My presence is my power."

Where are you experiencing the most significant roadblock? Are you clear on what you want but having a tough time taking action in the direction you know is best for you? If you feel called, use the following page to write down all that is coming up for you right now by reflecting on your current experiences.

A MOMENT FOR REFLECTION:

_____

_____

_____

_____

_____

_____

_____

_____

_____

_____

_____

_____

_____

_____

_____

Rise

"You can face everything and rise or forget everything and run. The choice is yours."
-Zig Ziglar

Chapter 4

RISING ABOVE

Choice is the one thing you have control over. In Chapter Three, I talked about the importance of clarity. When you can master the art of getting clear on what you want, you automatically place yourself on the path of rising above any obstacle that comes your way. It's important to note that all challenges and obstacles come with discomfort, depending on your level of conscious awareness and how far along you are on your journey. If you have experienced several seasons of bouncing back from challenging moments, chances are you have developed resilience and the ability to navigate storms with greater ease.

So, what if you are stuck in a rut right now? What can you do to shift from stagnancy to success, allowing you to move that needle in a positive direction? Chances are a subconscious limiting belief is coming up for you as fear. Feel the emotion, name it and bring it with you. The fear or limiting belief tries to stop you. You dissolve what is holding you back by placing your energy in motion. Action is the key element to unlock and align with your desired outcome.

You can talk yourself into something, or you can talk yourself out of something; the choice is yours. The more uncomfortable you allow yourself to get over time, the easier stepping into the unknown becomes. You are building your mental and emotional muscles, just as an athlete trains theirs for peak performance. Shift your focus to what can go right and not what can go wrong. The goal isn't necessarily to become "fearless" but "fear-driven," leaning into the fear, as it will exist on some level throughout your life, so allow fear to lead you. Show up, have faith, and watch all of those roadblocks open the way so you can elevate. Remember, even the most minor acts of courage will create monumental shifts toward success.

An Icon and an Alter Ego

Adele is a 16-time Grammy Award winner, has 18 *Billboard Music Awards*, and has 5 *American Music Awards*. She is among the most decorated singer-songwriters known for her powerful vocals and songwriting. She has made no secret of debilitating anxiety attacks and constant panicking on stage, stating, "The thought of an audience that big frightens the life out of me." So how did she break barriers and rise above to become one of the most beloved artists of our time? Adele has been candid in talking about how she gravitated toward a tactic that fellow sensation Beyoncé adopted—an alter-ego. Beyoncé becomes Sasha Fierce. It's a psychological hack backed by science where you distance your feelings from your behavior by assigning the feelings to a third person, in this case, an alter-ego. By doing so, Adele has detached herself from her fears, specifically her fear of rejection by her fans, by thinking how her alter-ego responds in such a situation. Beyoncé's Sasha Fierce would show up big and fierce to overcome any fear of performing.

There are many other methods one could use to overcome fear or any obstacles that are keeping you stuck and stagnant; here are a few that may help assist you in your process:

1. Cognitive Behavioral Therapy (CBT) is a form of psychological treatment that is effective for a range of issues, including depression, anxiety disorders, alcohol and drug abuse, severe mental illness, and eating disorders. CBT usually involves efforts to change thinking patterns, including:

- Learning to recognize distortions in thinking that are creating problems and then reevaluating them in a positive light.

- Facing fears instead of avoidance.

- Calming the mind and body—2 effective ways are:

  o *Self-regulation:* the ability to understand and manage your behavior and reaction to feelings and situations. It includes regulating reactions to strong emotions like frustration, excitement, anger, and embarrassment.

  o *Desensitization:* This technique is often used to treat various anxiety disorders, phobias, and post-traumatic stress disorder (PTSD). They can be effective in helping individuals overcome their fears and anxieties by reducing their emotional and physiological responses to the feared stimuli. However, it's important to note that desensitization should be conducted by qualified mental health professionals who can tailor the approach to the individual's specific needs and monitor their progress. The goal of desensitization is to make the person less sensitive or anxious when confronted with something that triggers distress or fear.

There are two main types of desensitization techniques:

- **Systematic Desensitization:** This approach was developed by behavioral therapist Joseph Wolpe in the 1950s. It involves gradual and systematic exposure to the feared stimulus or situation while simultaneously teaching the individual relaxation techniques. The process typically involves the following steps:

  a. *Relaxation Training:* The individual is taught relaxation techniques such as deep breathing, progressive muscle relaxation, or meditation to stay calm.

  b. *Creation of Hierarchy:* The therapist and the individual create a hierarchy of anxiety-provoking situations or stimuli related to the fear or phobia. These situations are ranked from the least anxiety-inducing to the most anxiety-inducing.

c. *Exposure:* The person is exposed to the least anxiety-provoking situation from the hierarchy while practicing relaxation techniques. Once they can do this without significant anxiety, they move on to the next item on the hierarchy and repeat the process until they can face the most anxiety-provoking situation without distress.

- **Flooding:** Another desensitization technique involves exposing the individual to the most anxiety-provoking situation or stimulus immediately rather than gradually. By facing the fear head-on, the person will eventually become habituated to the anxiety, and it will decrease. This approach can be intense and is typically conducted under the guidance of a trained therapist.

2. Clarity Breathwork—formerly known as rebirthing—is a robust process of healing and transformation. It deeply supports clearing old energies, patterns, conditioning, negative thoughts, and emotions and opens the doors wide for new life and greater consciousness. Most of us don't breathe fully; we hold back our breath and have been doing so for most of our lives. When we breathe fully and consciously, we can quickly release what we hold and open to an incredible expansion of consciousness, including greater forgiveness and self-love. This inner change brings about shifts in our outer lives for the better.

Clarity breathwork supports people in releasing stress and tension, healing and resolving trauma, gaining deeper insights into current life issues, and accessing their own internal healing energy, creativity, and inner knowing.

It helps to activate the subconscious mind and bring awareness and insights not easily accessed through traditional therapy. Breath opens the energy channels in the body and allows what we have been holding onto to surface and be released. This may be suppressed emotional material, physical blocks in the body, old beliefs, structures and identifications, old memories, fight/flight/freeze patterns, and addictions. Clarity breathwork combines counseling and insight and a somatic experiential process where clients gain a deep insight, release emotional baggage, and feel the patterns shifting and transforming at a deep cellular level.

I have used clarity breathwork in private sessions with a trauma timeline release facilitator, Sandra Rolus, whom I hold in the highest regard. My experience was profound, which brought up moments I completely forgot about as a young child and allowed me to release major subconscious blockages that I have been holding onto for decades. As a lifelong advocate of learning and growing, it should come as no surprise that I became a certified clarity breathwork practitioner to help others along their journey. I use this practice now in my Women's Sacred Wellness Experiences when needed; the results are miraculous when the client commits to the process and does the work. This is an excellent example of doing the inner work. It's not always pleasant, but it's worth it.

In my most significant breakthrough session, I cried and started shaking uncontrollably; my hands and fingers morphed into weird, deformed shapes that felt paralyzed in that form, my face and lips went numb, and my entire body felt like it was scorched with a match, lighting me up like I was on pins and needles. If I hadn't had my practitioner with me to facilitate the session, I would have given up since enduring that period of discomfort isn't something one can easily navigate alone. The amount of trauma and pain I was carrying on a cellular level was something I didn't think or feel was possible. Our logical minds can bury just about anything if we allow it, yet that is when the disease takes hold of us like prisoners of war. That period of being "uncomfortable" was worth every second to shed the emotional weight I was carrying to have a lifetime of openness and healing. Not only did clarity breathwork spring me into alignment, but it also blessed me with renewal and the opportunity to walk into this next chapter of my life feeling fully alive! For a quick reset on the spot, you can do a simple box breathing exercise which is breathing in fully for 4 seconds, holding at the top for 4 seconds, exhaling for 4 seconds then holding at the bottom for 4 seconds. Repeat this cycle 6-9 times and it will change your physiology instantly.

3. Stream-of-Consciousness Writing: I began using this free-flow technique in 2014, which helped immensely with purging my thoughts onto paper without structure or guidelines. Stream-of-consciousness writing is a powerful literary technique that allows writers to tap into their subconscious thought process and explore their innermost feelings, fears, and emotions without being constrained by structure and writing rules. And the good news is you don't have to be a professional writer to use this technique. Grab a pen, notebook, or piece of paper and begin your mental dump. Release every thought and feeling that comes to mind on paper. Your hand may cramp, but that's alright; take a quick break and get back into this cathartic and healing process. Authors who use this technique aim for emotional and psychological truth; they want to show a snapshot of how the brain moves from one place to the next. Thought isn't linear; you don't think in logical, well-organized, or complete sentences.

Here is an example of stream-of-consciousness writing:

"Movement it goes time flies by so fast that I want to breathe and let go with no worries I want to live and enjoy the birds chirping so beautifully my heart sings with joy and the green grass and the smell in the air all create beauty within me I want to do more live more be more…"

As I wrote this chapter, I took a moment to write in a stream of consciousness for this example. I only wrote what came to my mind through my thoughts and feelings at this very moment. I will have my editor leave it "as is" so you can see the lack of punctuation. This is a great practice, especially if you are experiencing any blockages or find yourself feeling overwhelmed by fear. I often find that fully surrendering to this free-flow technique becomes a spiritual moment. I am allowing spirit to move through me and onto the paper.

Reviewing many of these sessions, I know what came up was not from me but guidance from spirit. Some would describe it as God speaking to them; for me, this is interconnected. I have been writing consistently since 1999, so I know how my voice translates onto paper. When I show up in a stream-of-consciousness session, anything can come up. Therefore, I also use this technique often when going through challenging times.

Whatever method you choose, all the above options have helped many master any obstacle or fear-based thought and rise above. You will learn more techniques in the coming chapters to support this process.

Courage

"Courage starts with showing up and letting ourselves be seen."
- *Brené Brown*

Chapter 5

THE COURAGE TO BE YOU

Since this book is all about living in alignment so you can feel fully alive, I naturally had to touch on tapping into your authenticity, what makes you... well, you!

Living in your truth typically means living authentically and being true to yourself. It involves embracing your beliefs, values, and individuality and making choices that align with your genuine self, regardless of external pressures or expectations. When walking in your truth, you honor your thoughts, feelings, and aspirations. It involves being honest with yourself and others, embracing your strengths and weaknesses, and being open about who you are. This authenticity can lead to a more fulfilling and satisfying life because you're finally aligning with your genuine self. It's a journey that requires self-awareness, courage, and self-acceptance. This might involve examining your beliefs, understanding your motivations, and making choices that resonate with your core values.

You are the only one who can put this package together and get clarity on what that looks like because it is a process that stems from within. It's not coming from an external source. A question I always lead with is, "What does my heart say? Where do I feel the most alive when I'm in an experience?" And the follow-up question, "Who or what is adding value to my life, and who or what is not?" This is the purest form of explanation and confirmation received when I lead with these questions.

In regards to relationships, you can lead with, "What is working and what is not working" when reevaluating the situation rather than labeling it "bad or good." When I'm experiencing something and feel alive, I feel a buzzing sensation and goosebumps all over my body. It's important to note that this process is not to be confused with being uncomfortable or feeling fear because what is meant for you will often feel scary and risky. The most significant rewards often stem from summoning the courage and determination to forge your unique journey. Pay close attention to your environment and use that for guidance to understand more clearly what resonates with you. How does a specific person influence you and your decision making? Does it fuel your growth, or does the interaction take you further away from your core values? Your environment will have a significant impact on your life experience.

When you have the courage to be you and honor self, you will begin to make decisions that are for your highest and best good. We all have an inner compass, which serves as our guidance point. Trust it. Tapping into your inner knowing and learning to walk in your truth is a transformative journey that involves self-discovery, self-acceptance, and authentic living. And sometimes, to protect your peace, you have to adjust your proximity.

Here are several steps and practices that can help you in your quest to walk in your truth.

1. Reflection. Spend time reflecting on those values, beliefs, and aspirations and what matters most to you. Tap into that feeling and allow it to guide you. Pose a few self-discovery questions: "What are my strengths?" "What areas do I need more knowledge in to expand and grow?" This involves complete and utter honesty with yourself. We all know where our strengths and weaknesses lie and what those look like. Reflecting on those aspects allows you to understand yourself better. It's a process that takes time.

Grab a journal and start writing in that self-reflection mode, which will help guide you throughout the self-discovery process. Get to know yourself more intimately. Additional journal prompts that may assist you during your reflection and co-creative process are:

- Where is my ego influencing my heart and decision making?
- What attachments am I holding onto that are no longer serving me?
- Who do I need to forgive? (sometimes it is yourself.)
- What healthy boundaries do I need to reinforce or begin?
- How do I see myself living my best life? (Feel and picture yourself in the end result)

2. Explore your authenticity. Embrace it by accepting yourself as you are. Practice self-compassion by treating yourself as you would a dear friend or loved one. Understand that it's okay to have imperfections, quirks, and all these unique traits because that's what makes you who you are, and that's the beauty of being your own unique body. There is no one like you. Your body, voice, personality, and all the traits that make you. Over the years, I have mentored many entrepreneurs who initially adopted the mindset that their industry is too saturated, therefore they wouldn't be able to succeed, which is not the least bit true. It's a story they have created to be true. There is no one like you.

So, when you can embrace your authenticity and uniqueness, that's your power, and start honing in on that and growing yourself from the inside out. You will shine in a different light than somebody else, and everyone is attracted to certain personalities. Just focus on what you have control over, which is your growth and your abundant way of being, and you will align with those seeking who you are. Then double down on learning the skill sets required to additionally set you apart from the rest.

3. Identify your truth. Think about what feels genuine to you. Consider your passions, interests, and the things that make you feel most alive. Recognize your own voice and intuition amidst societal expectations or pressures. Another really important part of this process, something I learned over many years, is setting healthy boundaries. As many of you know, I am a former people pleaser.

Throughout my journey, I had to learn to set boundaries that are vital in walking and speaking your truth. Learn to establish boundaries that honor your needs and protect your authenticity. Boundaries can help maintain your emotional and mental well-being and ensure that you're not compromising your values or beliefs for the sake of others.

If you find yourself in a situation with an individual who has not committed to their own healing or growth journey, here is a quick blueprint for setting healthy boundaries:

- Identify the negative behavior and its impact on you. This awareness is crucial in understanding why boundaries are necessary. Begin to define your boundaries, getting clear on what behaviors and interactions are unacceptable or detrimental to your mental and emotional health. Specify what you will and won't tolerate, and communicate it clearly and assertively.

- Communicate your boundaries using statements like, "I feel uncomfortable when you speak to me in that manner. I need you to communicate respectfully, or this relationship will change." (Whatever that looks like to you.) Use language that feels right for you, and navigate the conversation lovingly, regardless of the other person's anger, manipulative tactics, or overpowering nature. If setting a boundary on your own feels unsafe, seek the support of a family member or friend. In extreme cases, you may need to hire a therapist or mediator to facilitate the communication of your boundaries.

During this process, it's really important to stand your ground and not waiver from the boundary you just set. Be firm and consistent. Once you've set boundaries, you have to maintain them. You are setting the foundation.

Often, it's family members with whom you need to establish and maintain boundaries. If they don't respect your personal standards, then there won't be a relationship. I know that may sound harsh; however, I have discovered that people who tend to say that are usually the ones who benefit from your lack of boundaries. If the other person or situation isn't in that same alignment, there's going to be conflict. There's going to be uneasiness and a constant push of "What can I still get away with?" It's up to you to be firm and consistent. Consistency is the most crucial part of this entire process because unhealthy individuals will always test boundaries to see what they can get away with. Stand firm and enforce the limits you've set. Then, you might have to limit interaction. It might involve spending less time with them or maintaining minimal contact to reduce their impact on your life. Along the way, it's really important to recognize manipulation tactics that toxic individuals might use to breach your boundaries. These come in forms of gaslighting, guilt-tripping, or other forms of manipulation that can erode your resolve. Stay vigilant, come back to self, come back to the reason why you are doing this in the first place. If you're noticing a pattern where people are not respecting your boundaries and they're just now using other means to try and get a rise out of you, then maybe it's time to completely distance yourself and remove yourself entirely from that person, situation, or environment. This would be in severe cases where boundaries are repeatedly violated, and the toxicity persists.

4. Self-Care. If you do not have a self-care practice at this point in your life, I encourage you, by all means, to please get started. I list many in this book. Take care of your mental and emotional well-being by practicing mindfulness, seeking support from loved ones who are healthy, engaging in healthy hobbies, or you may need to seek professional help, and that's okay. Everyone should have a therapist or some sort of counselor, whether a spiritual counselor, a mentor, or somebody who can guide you through the process. We're not expected to do it all on our own.

That's why community, connection and having relationships and deepening those relationships are paramount for a healthy, fruitful, and abundant life in all ways. Showing respect for yourself by nurturing every area of your being builds self-love. It will increase self-confidence, which will allow you to enforce healthy boundaries. It's all connected my friend.

These steps provide you with a quick framework to walk in your truth. If you are having a hard time establishing and holding firm to your boundaries, then my suggestion would be to connect with a facilitator who can help guide you along the path of your own healing journey. This way, you can learn how to show up for yourself and build self-confidence, which, in turn, will allow you to tap into your power so you can honor and respect yourself in moments when toxic individuals try to overstep. Take it from me, a former lifelong people pleaser (former being the keyword); I know this set-up all too well. My greatest accomplishments to date are not what others may think. It's the ability to honor, love, and respect myself so deeply that I no longer allow or entertain individuals who don't show up correctly.

It's also important to practice communication with yourself and others. Expressing your thoughts and feelings openly, while being considerate of others, is an essential part of walking in your truth. Cultivate mindfulness to stay connected with the present moment, practicing self-compassion by treating yourself with kindness and understanding, especially in moments of difficulty or vulnerability. Then, take action. Act in alignment with your values. Make decisions that resonate with your authentic self. Taking steps (even the smallest of ones) that reflect your truth can build momentum and confidence in your journey. And, of course, surround yourself with healthy support, people who accept you for who you are, and support your journey towards authenticity. Having a supportive network will encourage and reinforce your commitment to honoring yourself and your dedication for continuous learning and growth.

Understand that the journey to authenticity is ongoing. You must always be learning. You must always be growing so you are evolving to the next chapter in your life. Embrace change and adapt as you gain new insights and experiences. Remember, walking in your truth is a personal and unique journey. It's not a destination but a way of living. It's about accepting and embracing who you truly are and allowing that authenticity to guide your decisions and actions throughout your life.

Happiness is an inside job—it's a choice. It's possible to be happy during tough times. I've been there. I shift my focus towards the opportunity to grow and evolve. Think about it, when you look at every situation that's presented to you, it's an opportunity to grow. It's an opportunity to learn more, specifically, to learn more about yourself. That's the fun part. Then the hit doesn't become so brutal when something doesn't go your way; it doesn't take you down forever. It may push you back a little bit, and that's okay. That's part of feeling the feeling and then getting back up and moving through it. This is where you build resilience. This is how you build grit. Those are traits and characteristics that will always bring you through any season of your life. That's something that no one can ever take away from you.

The courage to be you isn't necessarily easy, yet when you continue to show up and pour into the beautiful human being you are, things begin to change. You get to experience life through a completely different lens—a lens of love and compassion.

Souls
Truth

"We are not the physical body we inhabit but are part of the infinite intelligence of all creation. When you summon the courage and heed that inner calling, listen to that infinite intelligence within, that's when your life begins to have purpose."
- *Dr. Wayne Dyer*

Chapter 6

UNRAVELING THE PROGRAMMING

Can you remember a time before all the programming began, before you took on thoughts, feelings, beliefs, and habits that were not yours? We all enter this world as pure and whole, and then life begins. We immediately take on our caregivers' thoughts and behaviors they learned throughout their upbringing, the positive and negative. Unless they healed any trauma or wounding, chances are that was passed onto you as well, through some form or another. This is when generational trauma occurs, yet the good news is that you can break the cycle and unchain from a timeline that is no longer serving you. The pathway to surrender and clearing can begin. This is an "unraveling" phase and an opportunity where your spiritual practices can allow for such healing and the ability to transmute any situation or judgment that may have occurred.

By committing to the process and consistently showing up to do the inner work needed to connect back to self, you shift into a new paradigm, a new way of being. You are shifting into a new state of being simply by utilizing self-love practices coupled with the power of letting go.

A question I believe is powerful to ask yourself is, *Who am I?* Let that sink in for a moment and feel into it with great curiosity. Who are you on a soul level? Everything you have been taught, from the way you speak to the traditions you engage in, have all been programmed in you since birth. Even if you felt different from your parents or siblings, chances are you conformed and accepted the "rules of the household" as a means of survival, seeking their love and approval. I'm inviting you to explore the depths of your being now. This is an opportunity to let all the labels and beliefs you hold disappear. We are going to unplug, reset, and reboot you. This chapter will allow you to dive deep into your soul's truth.

A Glimpse Into My Experience

I have immersed myself in deep, deep work throughout the years and have concluded that much of what I learned as a child was not in resonance with who I am at the soul level. I don't hold certain beliefs I learned as a young child, and some I do. This is not about casting judgments. As I mentioned in Chapter 1, I felt a lot of love growing up and deeply appreciate that my parents did their best with what they knew, yet I still formed habits and beliefs in my childhood that kept me from fully shining. The people-pleasing began early, as I felt loved and rewarded every time I helped more than any of my siblings. I would go above and beyond to make everyone happy at the expense of my happiness. I was constantly praised for pleasing people, so it continued. As time passed, it took a toll and came out as self-sabotage, making poor decisions and not setting a high personal standard. It's a cycle that would repeat for much of my young adult life.

This is an excellent example of how lacking self-worth, and poor self-esteem will keep you from not living in your soul's truth. I could feel it bubbling deep within, wanting to emerge like a freight train. I moved to Arizona in 1999 and began competing in fitness competitions. I was away from my entire family and circle of friends for the first time. I began focusing solely on myself: winning and placing in the top three at every competition, modeling in many fitness magazines, and writing content for noteworthy publications. It all seemed to go so well until it wasn't. The self-sabotage, coupled with passive-aggressive remarks from certain people, made its way back in, and slowly, I began to decline for a period of time. I quickly realized the power of a healthy environment specifically related to mindset and language.

My commitment to the process of self-discovery and personal development has always saved me, bringing me out of the trenches every time. My faith, while it had wavered for a bit in my early years, was always there, and I would lean into that space for comfort when I felt no one understood me or what I was going through. I knew I had to break the mental shackles and any subconscious beliefs that I had taken on as my own in order to rise above it all and become the woman I know I was put on this earth to be. God willing, I would be presented with many people and situations over time who would eventually become my greatest teachers, allowing me the grace and strength to evolve and dissolve any programming I had taken on along the way.

My life got better when I realized I no longer needed to live as the "nice" person, which only brought me stress, disrespect, and being taken advantage of due to my lack of healthy boundaries and pleasing manners. I became the "kind" person, living with intentionality, comfortable in "rocking the boat" a bit in order to engage in more authentic connections and a way of life. As I write this book, I feel free, and as my self-love continues to deepen and I make choices and decisions for my highest and best good, I feel more connected and aligned with who I am and where I am supposed to be. It's not about perfection but progress. I'm far from perfect; everyone is, contrary to popular ego.

The unlearning of all experiences that have not been in resonance with you is one of the most profound experiences in your life's journey. I've been able to release all that has not served me with love. Finding forgiveness through it all has allowed me to live in freedom while blazing out of the trenches and aligning with my life purpose and truth.

If you find yourself relating in any way and are trying to take the first step to shed the layers while unraveling the years of programming from your past, then allow me to guide you through several steps that gave me the courage to step into my power with greater clarity and self-love.

"You can't control how others interpret your words or actions. Everyone perceives situations based on their current mindset and beliefs. Stay in your lane. Show up in love, truth, integrity, and a pure heart. Stand boldly in your power, and all will align accordingly." - Chrissy May

How do you shift to a space that is in alignment with your authentic self, one that is going to bring you joy and fulfillment?

First and foremost, you must take action! If you are frozen in fear, you just need to get started. Even the smallest movement forward will create monumental shifts. Give yourself some grace along the way and allow the journey to unfold, messy moments and all. Consider the alternative if you choose not to accept this calling: You remain tired, confused, anxious, angry, resentful, drained, broke, annoyed, overwhelmed, and depressed. What do you have to lose in parallel to all of these low vibrational, self-loathing feelings? In my observation, absolutely nothing! It's time to listen to that little voice inside you, known as your inner guidance system. This is your soul calling you. Your inner compass wants to guide you. You have an opportunity to accept the call; don't hang up this time. Allow the old programming to die in order for the new to be born into existence.

Many of my faith-based readers will be able to relate this to being "born again." When you hear the term "born again Christian," it is an expression many use to define the moment or process of fully accepting faith in Jesus Christ. It is an experience when the teachings of Christianity and Jesus become real, and the "born again" acquire a personal relationship with God.

In the Bible, the reference is made in 1 Peter 1:3 - *"In his great mercy, he has given us new birth into a living hope through the resurrection of Jesus Christ."*

This signifies a spiritual renewal, forgiveness of sins, new life in Christ, and eternal life with God in heaven. Consider this as a transformation of the soul and heart by the works of the Holy Spirit.

Regardless of your belief system, you can draw upon a higher power to tap into while navigating this process. My faith gave me, and continues to provide me, with an unwavering love that is not found anywhere else. Lean into it and allow it to lead you out of what is no longer serving you. If you choose not to make this shift in your life, then you will continue to play the part of an actor, reading from a script in order to navigate the day-to-day. You will continue to feel that you are not in resonance with your true self. You will continue to just exist until one day, it's too late—because we all have an expiration date. That, my friends, is the one common fact we all share: an expiration date from this earthly plane.

So, what are you waiting for? There is nothing to lose, only a new lease on life to gain, and a magical one at that!

Steps You Can Take Right Now to Live in Your Soul's Truth

1. **Interrupt the pattern.** Locate one thing you can do today that you normally wouldn't do or say. When you show up for yourself, you shed old ways and habits that are no longer

serving you. This could be a different decision on what you eat, taking a walk, going to the gym, driving a different route to work, beginning to search for a job or career path that lights your soul on fire, whatever that looks like for you. It's a start. Commit to whatever this one thing is and see it through. Now, you have proven that you can show up for yourself and do what you say you will do. Focus on just one thing so you don't get overwhelmed. This step shifts you out of the pattern that keeps you stuck.

2. **Speak up**. Start having tough conversations with the friendships that are no longer in resonance with you or that family member or significant other who is constantly complaining, bringing you down, and maybe even abusive in how they speak to you. Having tough conversations, creating healthy boundaries, and sticking to them will align you with your soul's truth. You will feel liberated moving through this step. Do it scared, with your voice and knees shaking. You have set a new standard when you voice your truth. It is up to the other person to react or respond. This is not your issue any longer. It's a boundary being placed so you can align with your authenticity. If you feel worried about your safety, seek professional help and guidance in navigating this process. Do not enter into this on your own.

3. **Get connected.** Connect with a group, coach, therapist, or mentor to hold you accountable and help guide you when you feel yourself settling, falling back into the program that

kept you stuck and stagnant. It doesn't matter who or where you are; we all need a significant source of accountability when experiencing change, especially on the spiritual and emotional levels. They also may have insights and professional training to provide you with the tools and skill set to navigate this process easily.

4. **Make a commitment.** Commit to your spiritual practices that will support you along this transition and journey. That looks like spending more time in nature, connecting with yourself in meditation, clarity, breathwork, visualization, journaling, prayer, sound healing, yoga, ecstatic dance, water therapy, and reiki healing. These all have supported me, especially during *the dark night of the soul.* I wouldn't have been able to shift beyond the pain if it weren't for these practices and my relationship with God. Deepening these practices has allowed me the courage and confidence to transcend central limiting beliefs deeply suppressed in my subconscious mind and body. I encourage you to create your own and fully surrender to the healing process. Notice and give gratitude for the gift of peace these all bring along the way. Even the tiniest of improvements will keep guiding you in a positive direction. Stay consistent, and you will reap the rewards they all provide.

5. **Change your environment.** Be intentional with who, what, and where you allow yourself to be and what information you consume. If you seek a healthier environment, you need

to surround yourself with those in a healthy space who are committed to their growth process. The worst decision you could make is to stay in the same environment that made you stuck in the first place. Stagnancy stifles growth, so get moving! Locate your like-minded and like-hearted tribe and get connected.

The above steps are simple, yet it will take courage and discipline to maintain, especially in the beginning. Reflecting on my journey, I see that it was messy at moments and often painful; however, I was still evolving and shedding the layers that were no longer serving me. I was shifting and changing, and those who benefited from my lack of boundaries didn't like the *new* version of me because they could no longer get away with their manipulation and poor behavior. I set a new standard; I raised the bar of what is and is not acceptable. You will find many who stay stuck in the past, constantly referencing how you used to be, to make themselves feel better because they have yet to show up and do the work. Allow the ship to sink. Rebuild your foundation stronger and healthier than ever before, and you will call in those that are of the same vibration as you. You will align with the right people, places, and opportunities. Sit with the above steps and journal areas in your life right now that apply.

Additionally, ask yourself, *What old programs am I holding onto that are no longer in resonance with who I am?* Spend time working through every detail. Be specific so you can release with ease. In the next chapter, I will provide techniques that will allow you to reprogram and reframe your mindset so you can experience a new reality that aligns with your soul's truth.

Create

"The key to turn our
dreams into reality
is action."
- *Jim Rohn*

Chapter 7

CREATING YOUR NEW REALITY

Your Thoughts and What You Speak
Will Create Your Reality

I've been fascinated by the power of mindset and positive thinking since I was a teenager. It initially began when I wanted to learn how to strengthen my mind as a competitive figure skater. How did Kristi Yamaguchi or Michelle Kwan go on the ice and perform at such a high level, consistently over time and under intense moments of pressure? I pinpoint these two decorated champions as they were figure skating's elite competitors during my training era. I understood the on-ice training aspect, yet even some of the world's most talented skaters would buckle under pressure.

I needed to learn how to keep my mind strong during my performances, so I began reading *The New Toughness Training for Sports* by James Loehr, Ed.D., a world-renowned performance psychologist. Many books followed my pursuit, such as *The Power of Positive Thinking* by Norman Vincent Peale and *The Power of*

Now by Eckhart Tolle. These three books would serve me well as a skater, a few years later as a fitness competitor, and in my early years as a business owner. They would be the catalyst for my lifelong personal development journey.

"She's so lucky!"

If I had a dollar for every time I heard this statement, I would have an additional stream of income pouring in. Those who don't understand the power of thought and expressed words will continue to find themselves in a negative loop, referencing how everyone else is "lucky" when abundance pours in or good things go their way. This is an example of a poor mindset and one playing "victim" to their life experiences. As I have mentioned a few times in this book, we all have a choice of how we choose to show up for ourselves and what daily habits we will create to live an abundant life. Early, I adopted a lens of *what is possible* in life and became a lifelong student of aligning accordingly to receive. Luck is a rarity, yet intentionality determines the experience of your desires. If you genuinely desire success, you must be clear and intentional about pursuing it. Become purposeful in your plan, bringing you closer to what you want to experience. You attract who you are, not what you want, so you embody what you want to bring into existence, thus creating your new reality.

When I chose to become something great, even though I lacked training and experience at the beginning, I knew that my willingness to see it as possible, coupled with following through with repetitive action and perseverance, eventually made it possible. This so-called luck was my clear vision coupled with a consistent action plan, two decades of working with clients, and my life experiences; I can confidently say that luck rarely has anything to do with it. I've worked with many investors in real estate over the years, and I hear repeatedly how they got "lucky" in certain markets. Yet, they had the confidence and clarity to take that calculated risk and reap the reward. The good news is that this is available to anyone who wants to create a new reality for themselves; if it were indeed purely "luck," then that would show separation, and we are not separate from creation; we are one. Shift your thoughts, shift your life. The choice is yours.

It's important to understand that your brain responds to two things: the pictures you make and the words you speak. It learns by repetition, specifically in the present tense. You can create a new reality simply by mastering what you think and speak.

It requires reframing negative thought patterns that disable you and keep you stuck. You live what you learn, so if you grew up in an environment that wasn't uplifting, chances are you still operate from those thought patterns and speech. The key is to unlearn everything so you can reprogram your mind accordingly. Think of it as swiping a computer or phone of all the information stored on it, rebooting it, and simply uploading new information. That is what you will be implementing to achieve a new reality. So, let's rewrite your story. It would help if you changed the beliefs you have that are associated with your story from a disempowering belief to an empowering belief.

Allow me to go first and provide an example.

When I reflect on my adoption as a little baby, I intuitively knew from a very young age that I was meant to be with my parents, who adopted me at three months old. My experience is not the norm. I have spoken to many adoptees who have felt abandoned by their birth mother and crushed that she would give them up. That is a disempowering belief. While that feeling is valid, as an adult, there is an opportunity to shift that to an empowering belief. Reframing that would look like, "I'm grateful for the gift of life and blessed that I was released to experience what it means to be loved and cared for."

In my situation, I have always felt gratitude to my birth mother for choosing to give me up to a family that could provide a stable and healthy environment, one that she could not fulfill. It could have gone sideways for me. She could have allowed me to grow up in a toxic environment, and who knows how that would have unfolded. I view it as an act of love and ultimate selflessness to give up a baby she carried in her womb for nine months. I saw the good.

I understand many of you reading this won't relate to being adopted, so I will provide several examples of reframing that have helped my clients shift their mindset from negative to empowering.

Reframing the Way You Perceive and Interpret Situations

Disempowered belief: "What if I regret this?"

Empowered belief: "What if this sets me free?

Disempowered belief: "I'm not good enough."

Empowered belief: "I am constantly learning and growing. I can achieve greatness through effort and persistence."

Disempowered belief: "I'm a failure because I made a mistake."

Empowered belief: "Mistakes are opportunities to learn and improve. I can use this experience to become better and more resilient."

Disempowered belief: "I can't; it's just how I am."

Empowered belief: "I have the power within to change and improve. I can develop new habits, skills, and perspectives to create a more positive and fulfilling life."

Disempowered belief: "I'm too old to pursue my dreams."

Empowered belief: "It's never too late. Each stage of life brings opportunities, and I can create anything I want in any season of life I desire."

Disempowered belief: "I am always unlucky."

Empowered belief: "I create my luck through positive actions, learning more, becoming more intentional in my lifestyle choices, and understanding I can turn any challenge into an opportunity."

Disempowered belief: "I missed out on opportunities because of my financial background."

Empowered belief: "While I faced challenges, my experiences gave me a unique perspective and a deep appreciation for opportunities. I can use this perspective to my advantage now in the present moment and align myself accordingly to exercise the next opportunity."

Disempowered belief: "He or she cheated on me."

Empowered belief: "Infidelity is a choice they made, and it doesn't diminish my worth. I am valuable and deserving of a healthy, committed relationship."

Disempowered belief: "Others are more attractive or fit than me."

Empowered belief: "Comparing myself to others doesn't serve me. I have unique qualities that make me attractive. There is no one like me, and that is my superpower."

Recognizing and challenging disempowering beliefs is the first step toward fostering a more positive and empowering mindset, allowing you to think better thoughts. See this quick framework on how the process works:

Thoughts → Create your feelings

Feelings → Create your actions/behavior

Actions/Behavior → Creates your outcome/event

This is the essence of cognitive reframing. Changing your thoughts will profoundly impact your emotions and behaviors, creating a new reality.

Depending on where you are on your journey, this simple process does not have to take a long time. You can experience a shift almost instantly! Consistency is vital to embody this practice fully. Below is a quick roadmap to reference.

Use This 5-Step System to Guide You Along the Way

1. Identify the negative thought pattern.

2. Challenge the negative thought and reframe.

3. Create additional positive affirmations to follow up this new belief, focusing on your strengths, achievements, and the positive qualities you possess.

4. Practice Gratitude. Focus daily on what is going right and not what is going wrong. This mindset shift will allow you to hold a higher level of thought.

5. Focus on solutions. Don't dwell. Pivot. Break down your challenge into manageable steps, then take action in a new direction.

I worked with a young woman for six months who was experiencing symptoms of depression, anxiety, and very low self-worth. While she wasn't diagnosed with any disorder by a psychiatrist, she felt lifeless and had a desire to experience a zest for life again. She knew the path she was heading down was not serving her. Her awareness allowed her to see the negative patterns she took on as her own, creating her current reality. After evaluating her lifestyle, I created a program similar to my fitness client, who went through an abusive marriage, coupled with the above cognitive reframing protocol. Her most significant pain point was social media, which is for many young adults these days, yet many don't even realize its impact on them until they remove it entirely. Within two weeks of being off all social media, her anxiety was nearly gone; at four weeks, she felt confident again and had clarity. It wasn't just her emotional state that shifted; her facial features also changed. She was glowing. We worked together for an additional five months as she wanted the accountability, and I also helped her launch a business she wanted to get off the ground for years, yet she could never find the energy.

I have seen dozens of men and women stuck in situations that most physicians would prescribe a pill for. Your environment, how you speak to yourself, and the negative thought patterns circling on repeat keep you stuck and stagnant. You have an opportunity every day to choose again. You hold the power within to shift the trajectory of your life simply by creating healthier thoughts. This process is available to everyone.

Trigger Alert:

If you are broke, depressed, out of shape, or addicted to unhealthy habits, it is 100% because of the choices you made and are currently making. If you are stuck, you are choosing to remain stuck.

Make today the day you choose again. You will create space to feel better even if you simply reframe the way you think, no longer playing the victim. That's a win! Focus only on that for a period, and it will keep stacking day after day, eventually leading you down a path you once only dreamed of. It will provide you the energy to take action and show up differently, thus providing you with better outcomes and experiences. If you are struggling to do it alone, that's okay! We are not meant to do life alone. Reach out and seek the help of a mentor, coach, friend or therapist. I would not be where I am today without the assistance of the above. It would be impossible. I chose not to buy designer purses and shoes for an extended period, choosing instead to invest in myself. I became a master at delayed gratification in that area.

I make no exaggeration when I say I have easily spent over $100,000 in the past several years on personal development, courses, and coaching. I know many people who spend that on material possessions to feel good or look the part because they hire me when they realize that isn't the solution. It's an inside job, my friends. Choose to do the inner work. Commit to showing up for yourself, and I promise you, Heaven on Earth will be the new reality that awaits. You must be intentional in your life.

I speak from experience through my struggles and the ability to overcome them. The most common excuse I have heard over the past 25 years is, "I don't have the money." Again, take an honest look at your current lifestyle and choices. I have yet to meet someone who couldn't find the money if they truly desired to get unstuck. This is where you can write need vs. want. Start making your food at home, stop buying alcohol, stop grabbing $5+ coffees every morning, stop buying your kids toys every week, pick up a side hustle for extra cash, and watch YouTube videos on how to learn something new that you can then create a side hustle to earn more money. The list goes on and on. The possibilities are endless when you shift your focus on solutions vs. problems.

Marisa Peer is a five-time bestselling author and creator of Rapid Transformational Therapy® (RTT). In addition, she is a nutritionist, relationship therapist, hypnotherapist trainer, and motivational speaker. Marisa uses hypnosis for anxiety, weight loss, addiction, and overcoming fear. She has spent over 30 years working with royalty, rock stars, actors, professional and Olympic athletes, CEOs, and media personalities. She has developed her own style, frequently called "life-changing."

I've experienced powerful results using Marisa's techniques, so naturally, I am studying to become a Rapid Transformational Therapist to incorporate this method into my practice and the wellness retreats I facilitate for women.

One of Marisa's brilliant techniques, which she created, is called the DICCC technique. It enabled her to beat cancer not just once, but twice.

This has to be one of the most incredible stories I have ever heard when speaking about the power of our mind. Marisa could command her body to heal. She decided not to allow the doctor's diagnosis in and focused on healing. The power of her words and thoughts she kept healed her body.

The words she spoke, visualized, and felt are:

D - I direct

I - I instruct

C - I command

C - I compel

C - I code

"I direct, instruct, command, compel, and code my body to heal perfectly and properly, just as nature intended it to be right now."

She used this phrase over and over every single day. The keywords are at the end, "right now." Keeping it in the present tense. What is expected, tends to be realized.

I encourage you to begin your reframing of a new reality right now. The moment I began taking ownership of every experience in my life, I placed myself into an entirely new reality. One filled with abundance and joy. One of my favorite quotes by the late Wayne Dyer is, "If you change the way you look at things, the things you look at change." It's a mindset shit. You create your reality with the thoughts you think.

Power Practices

"Whatever we plant in our subconscious mind and nourish with repetition and emotion, will one day become a reality."
- *Earl Nightingale*

Chapter 8

POWER PRACTICES

As a lifelong student of personal development and growth, I have been able to formulate what has worked for me over two decades. From my first book on mental toughness in 1995 to my most recent read on the pathway of surrender and every book in between, all have provided me with insights, knowledge, and inspiration to carve out a plan that resonates with me, springing me into alignment. The practices I have incorporated over the years have shifted along the way, and for good reason—I keep growing! I learned this journey is unique for all who choose to walk it. There are extreme highs and dark lows along the way, but the rewards are plentiful, and the unraveling of who you once were to who you are becoming is an exquisite experience, one I have fallen in love with.

There are thousands of books on "self-help," and it is not a one-size-fits-all protocol. I've found that I take little golden nuggets from each and decide if I need them or hang them up on my mental shelf and use them later. This is what I would love for you to take away from this book and the info I have shared. Maybe there is a highlight or two that you resonated with and will begin using immediately, or you can get back to it in the future when you feel in resonance. Whatever that looks like for you, know that you are the co-creator of your life. You decide what ingredients are in the recipe and then bake or cook as you like. I'm merely sharing processes proven to work for myself and clients over the past twenty years. This beautiful life we are given is a gift, providing infinite possibilities.

The Art of Embodiment

Spiritual embodiment refers to integrating spiritual practices, awareness, and experiences into one's physical body, daily life, and overall being. It involves aligning one's spiritual beliefs and practices with the tangible, lived experience of the body. Spiritual embodiment is a journey of integration, mindfulness, and conscious living that seeks to unite existence's physical and spiritual dimensions. For many, it involves a connection with a higher power; mine is God, while others use the term "universe." This connection is a guiding force, providing a sense of purpose and meaning in life. My personal experiences are proof enough for me that God indeed exists, and it's a debate I don't engage in with anyone. If you believe in a different higher power, bless your heart; I make no judgments.

My spiritual practices began as a little girl. The first was prayer. I fondly remember bedtime prayers with my mom. I can recall so many still to this day. The power of prayer is real. I've experienced moments when I shouldn't be here writing this book. I've witnessed miracles take place and diseases cured. Prayer is not solely for asking; I sit in prayer throughout the day, giving thanks for the simplicity of being alive. To have another opportunity to live, create, connect, and experience. My daily conversations with God are precious and fulfilling. When I receive those miracle moments in small or big winks, I know my faith fosters a deeper connection between the spiritual and physical world.

Additional spiritual practices include meditation, yoga, sound healing, reiki, and breathwork. I use it all for mental and emotional well-being. Besides daily prayer, the most significant impact I've experienced is breathwork. Embodied breathwork provides a platform for self-discovery and self-expression. Breath becomes a tool for uncovering more profound layers of oneself. I have had powerful breakthroughs in my breathwork practice.

I've created a blueprint of "8 Power Practices" that will help you shift the trajectory of your life. They will all help you deepen self-love, gain clarity, and guide you to living in your soul's truth.

The Power of 8

1. Sound Healing Meditation: Elevate your meditation experience with the addition of sound vibrations that allow for healing on a cellular level. I love this practice for renewal, balance, clarity, removing blockages, and fostering a greater connection with your body and the world around you. This practice involves cultivating embodied awareness, presence, and a sense of interconnectedness.

I've used this practice with clients experiencing health challenges or diseases to fight off infection and visualize healing.

Overall, this is a powerful practice to decrease anxiety, fear, and stress. You will feel more peaceful, happy, and calm. Sound waves stimulate the parasympathetic nervous system, which slows the heart rate, reduces blood pressure, and activates healing in the body. Commit to a daily practice, which will also aid in reducing inflammation and boost the immune system. There are many ways to experience meditation. I've noticed that by adding sound therapy, I can go deeper, thus allowing for a more impactful result. If you can't access a facilitator or class in your area, play one off YouTube that resonates with you. My favorite is Mei-lan Maurits, a Dutch music artist who is exquisite.

2. Grounding, or Earthing: A therapeutic technique involving touching the Earth barefoot or lying down. The Earth's natural electric charge stabilizes physiology at the deepest levels - reducing inflammation, pain, and stress and improving blood flow, energy, sleep, and overall well-being. It's as simple as taking your shoes off and walking barefoot outdoors. I use this practice daily, and when I don't, I notice a difference! A while back, I was going through a highly stressful season of life. My body was experiencing tremendous strain, and I knew something wasn't right. My initial reaction was to drive myself to the emergency room, mainly out of fear, yet I received a loud message that said, *Go outside, bare feet, and turn your face to the sun.* Within seconds, I could feel my body stabilize by realigning my nervous system with Earth's powerful energy.

All of my clients use this practice and have also experienced profound results. Do you know what the best part of this is? It's accessible to all who choose to incorporate it into their practice. So, get outside, walk in the grass, feel the soil beneath your feet, or throw your toes in the sand. However, you choose to go about it, tune out the noise, and get grounded.

3. Intermittent Fasting: You may be surprised to find this in the list of power practices, yet fasting holds many physical, mental, emotional, and even spiritual benefits. I've been using intermittent fasting for years, and it has changed my life. It aids brain health and supports heart health, blood sugar levels, and circadian rhythm. Additionally, it improves gut health, influences metabolism, helps prevent diseases, delays aging, reduces anxiety, and helps with weight management. I've even noticed enhanced clarity and focus when fasting. Connection to the source (God) becomes more apparent. Intuition is heightened. Everyone's body is different, so consult your practitioner on the proper protocol. I do a 16:8 fast (a food restriction for sixteen hours, with a window of eight hours to eat). This period worked for me, yet it took me a month to figure out what worked best. It would help to stay hydrated by drinking plenty of clean, filtered water. I also drink from glassware instead of plastic to avoid toxic chemicals leaking into the water. The amount of water you should drink depends on your body weight.

The formula to help you determine the number of ounces of water is to multiply your weight by .7 (body weight x .7) If you live in hotter climates. This will increase. During my window of food consumption, I focus on lean, organic, grass-fed protein, organic vegetables, and fruit. Stay away from sugar and processed foods. Keep it simple.

4. Making Vows: Do what you say you are going to do. Keep the commitments you make with yourself. You can show up and do hard things. One of my all-time favorite Bible verses is, *"I can do all things through Christ who strengthens me."* (Philippians 4:13). Tap into your higher power, feel the oneness and support. I have experienced many highs and lows throughout my life, and I can connect the dots and notice a pattern that thunders. When I am not in harmony by keeping my commitments, life will mirror that. Others stop showing up for me like I would want them to, plans get canceled, and opportunities fall through.

The quickest way to build confidence and resilience is to do hard things that are uncomfortable. Five weeks before my dad passed in 2022, my mom was diagnosed with cancer. My world shifted overnight. The pain I felt was deep, yet I knew this was not a time to throw in the towel and lose myself, yet face it head-on and move through the pain. After six rounds of chemo, a successful surgery, and by the grace of God, my mom is thriving today. Her warrior spirit and faith were inspiring, especially during the passing of her husband of fifty years. It gave me inspiration and a desire to step my life up. I wanted to squeeze even more out of life, and I knew the only way was to force myself to get uncomfortable.

Every season of life will demand a different you. I was exiting out of hermit season and into a season of excellence. I committed to and completed the 75 Hard Challenge by Andy Frisella, a strict mental toughness program requiring you to complete specific tasks daily. If you miss one task, you have to start over at day one. This challenge became the springboard that allowed me to show up fully during a difficult season of life! It proved I can do hard things and get through tough times. I encourage everyone to consider at least one round of it. Since then, I have continued to show up in grand ways. My vow to myself and seeing it through, regardless of what was unfolding in my outer world, has permitted me to shine personally and professionally. The most valuable gift it provided was the love I gave myself. My self-worth and self-love are at an all-time high. Do hard things. Build yourself from within, and you will navigate life with grace.

5. Letting Go: Have you ever tried so hard to make something happen only for it not to work out how you intended? I know I have. I also know the more I trust the process, the better the outcome. Have faith in your journey, even during challenging times. Use the reframing technique I shared in the previous chapter to release any fear or anxiety about letting go. The one constant in life is that everything changes. Strengthening your practice of letting go allows you to live fully in the present moment. My present became a genuine gift when I surrendered and released my past! Can you imagine the toll on my overall well-being if I held onto the abusive relationship I endured in my twenties? Or the passing of my dad?

Letting go and choosing a healthier thought allows a transition for new beginnings. It's the next chapter in my book of life. When my dad passed, I moved through that debilitating pain and eventually viewed it with a lens of love. I thanked God for giving me the time I had with him. Every experience, labeled "good" or "bad," allows us to receive and grow. I am not saying it's easy but possible; and the easier you can flow through the ever-changing current of life, the more delicious the journey becomes. I am keenly aware of how brief this human experience is, so I have sharpened this practice to avoid missing out on the miracle of life. If you are going through a divorce, break-up, loss of job, passing of a loved one, a diagnosis, or financial hardship, you are not alone.

We all experience moments of pain and struggle throughout our lifetime. Often, you can't control what happens, yet you can control how you respond. Pain is inevitable—suffering is optional. I choose to give it to God and allow space for healing and growth. Become intentional; be specific. Feel all the feelings coming up for you, witness them, and then release them. Resistance keeps the feeling active.

By letting go, the energy behind the feeling dissipates. The key to letting go is to release the thoughts and get out of your monkey mind, which only activates the feeling that keeps you stuck. The practice of letting go provides freedom. Your only job here is to choose a better thought. Reframe the way you speak. Shift your focus on the present moment. Grounding and sound healing meditations assist in this process. It took me years to fully surrender, and often, I catch myself wanting to control every outcome like before, so I pivot and shift my focus to writing, dancing, exercising, hiking, or walking. Making a positive energy shift is the quickest way to pop yourself back into the present moment, allowing space for the miracle to occur.

6. Serving: Contribution to the well-being of others with no attachment or personal gain can create a life of abundance simply through service and kindness. This practice can be challenging for those who have nothing to give; that is not true, however. If you are financially strained, you have the gift of your time. I talk a lot about intentionality. Everyone is given the same 24 hours daily, yet not all spend it wisely. Turn off the TV and call or meet up with someone going through a tough time. Cook for a family who needs the support. Take a walk and perform random acts of kindness to strangers on the street. Walk your neighbor's dog. Offer free babysitting for a friend. Serving goes beyond giving money. It's easy to cut a check if you are financially abundant; it takes more energy to offer your time, but the reward is more significant.

Human connection creates a long-lasting bond. I like to break bread with friends and make new connections. There is something special about eating lunch or dinner together and engaging in meaningful conversation. I like to pick up the tab without hesitation and treat them for no reason other than appreciation for our time together. I've mentored hundreds of people over the years. When I had my fitness company, I offered financially challenged individuals an opportunity to train with me for 3-4 months, all pro bono. It's in giving that we truly receive.

Through our love, generosity, and acts of kindness to others, we elevate the collective by inspiring others to do the same, creating a ripple effect in society. This powerful and transformative practice can change the trajectory of your life and all involved. If you feel stuck in a rut or going through a tough season of life, this practice will boost your mental health! The health benefits of secreting "feel good" chemicals include serotonin, which regulates your mood; dopamine, which gives you a sense of pleasure; and oxytocin, which creates a sense of connection with others. Giving can stimulate your brain's mesolimbic pathway or reward center while releasing endorphins. Serving others will set you free. Enjoy!

7. Forgiveness. This is an ongoing practice, and the rewards extend beyond personal well-being, positively impacting relationships and contributing to a more compassionate and interconnected world. Forgiveness does not condone poor behavior. Instead, it releases you from the shackles that keep you stuck in anger and resentment. I learned this many years ago, and I am grateful I have been able to master this practice. Forgiveness has been my saving grace through callous times. Forgiveness has given me a freedom I would have never known prior. It's allowed me to cultivate compassion and empathy, understanding that we all have imperfections and are subject to mistakes or poor choices.

Forgiving is the pathway to peace. It offers a more joyous life experience. I have been able to sit in silence without worry due to learning the art of forgiveness. What do I mean by that? If another person has spoken ill of me, passed judgment, wrongfully accused, or any other act that imposes hurt, I can sit with it, choose to forgive them for their acts, and eventually move on.

As I mentioned in the above practice of letting go, it's a choice to harbor anger and resentment, and my choice to let it go and forgive allows me the space and freedom to move on and choose again. I have been known to "thank" the individual for exposing their shadow side. The quicker someone exposes their truth, the less they waste my precious time. So, when you reframe the act of hurt that was done, you can see it is a gift. This all ties into self-love and living in your soul's truth. When you arrive at this glorious place, it is easy to forgive, pivot, and move on to what is meant for your highest and best good. You can then create space and align accordingly.

8. Prayer. You know by now that I am a big advocate of prayer. Many find solace, guidance, and connection through prayer. It serves as a source of comfort and strength. Even scientific studies have shown that prayer positively affects mental and physical well-being. How you pray is entirely up to you. There is no one set protocol to pray. It is a deeply personal and subjective experience. I respect all diverse beliefs and perspectives. Over the years, prayer is the very practice that has brought me immense comfort and connection. I love my daily conversations with God. My faith is unwavering even during painful moments, which require courage and trust, but it offers a life full of purpose and fulfillment. Sing praise to the Creator of the heavens and Earth for no reason other than you are grateful for this human experience and all the many colorful moments it brings.

I choose to glorify God through prayer and give thanks. Reflecting on the beautiful world created for humanity brings tears to my eyes. The simple fact that we are on a moving, rotating planet in the middle of the universe is awe-inspiring. Sitting in prayer daily will allow you to experience a connection that will provide answers if you listen. Yes, prayer provides solutions. It may not be what you always want to hear, yet when you walk in faith, you lead with the understanding that all is happening for you.

Many call this experience being divinely guided. You trust in a higher power to light your path. There is a song that comes to mind as I write this. It's by Jeremy Camp, who sings, *"I will walk by faith, even when I can not see because this broken road prepares your will for me."* When navigating hardship and heartbreak, this can provide strength and comfort while allowing alternate perspectives and miracles to unfold.

New Beginnings

"Can you trust that it is all happening
this way for a reason and that reason
is for your greatest expansion?
Can you trust that you are already
on the path leading you to a place
beyond your wildest dreams?"
- *Ashmi Pathela*

Final Thoughts

I chose to stop at eight chapters for many reasons. It symbolizes new beginnings, infinity, resurrection, abundance, inner stability, harmony, and embracing personal power toward enlightenment. By reading this book in its entirety, it is impossible for you not to experience a positive shift. Gaining clarity and understanding are key components in allowing space for self-love. Your awareness from the initial programming to now unlearning everything will provide you with a blank canvas to reframe and rewrite your story, one that is in alignment with your soul's truth. You hold the power within to create a new narrative.

I encourage you to open the floodgates and release all that is not serving you. You will build a new foundation by incorporating the many practices I have provided throughout this book and the tools you can gain to give you the courage necessary to take the first step. Every day is an opportunity to make changes; to do what your soul is calling you to do, no matter what someone else has to say about it. Leaning into what your body is telling you and making decisions based on what is authentically right for you. Taking leaps into the unknown that may not make sense, but you know in your heart are right. The portal to that quantum leap in your life is through the parts of yourself that you avoid. I pray you choose to accept the invitation to live a big, bold, and beautiful life.

Connect with Chrissy

Listen and follow the *Aligned + Alive* Podcast!

Available on all podcast platforms

Apple QR Code

Aligned + Alive Podcast

ChrissyMay.com

I appreciate your interest in my book and value your feedback as it helps me improve future versions of this book. I would appreciate it if you could leave your invaluable review on Amazon.com with your feedback. Thank you!

Enjoy this free guided meditation to elevate your life now!
Scan with your phone camera to open and listen.

Click below.

Made in the USA
Middletown, DE
03 September 2024